Journey of Faith

Adult Devotional

Dr. Derrick L. Randolph Sr.

DEDICATION

I dedicate this book to my family, Sharon Randolph, Derrick L. Randolph Jr. and Joshua Isaiah Randolph

Copyrighted Material

Introduction

Journey of Faith

The Journey of Faith

Receiving God's Revelation

Personal relationship with God

Knowing God's Scriptures

Walking in Grace

Life in God's Church

Daily Deliverance

Receiving God's Salvation

Developing Discipline

Knowing God

Loving Obedience

Learning about God

Suffering Affliction

Glory

I have outlined the Journey of Faith, using the ascent and descent of Mount Sinai. As we go up, we navigate through the process of spiritual development where we are receiving God's revelation. As we go down Mount Sinai, we are developing a personal relationship with God.

There are various stages along the journey and lessons to walk through. The Journey of Faith Adult Devotional features:

- The Bible (Scripture)

- A Prophetic Word *(Adult devotional to inspire and edify the faith)*

- Self-Reflection *(Adult reflection questions)*

- Adult Journal *(Section for adults to share their thoughts)*
- A Prophetic Point *(1 phrase short summary)*
- Prayers and poems

We wish God's grace and peace to you. We hope you are blessed by the Journey of Faith. Here are the Instructions

1. Read the *Biblical stories and scriptures.*

2. Read the ***Prophetic Word*** and ***Self-Reflection.***

3. Complete the ***Adult Journal.***

4. Close with the **Prophetic Point, Prayers,** *and* **Poems.**

Part 1 - Receiving God's Revelation

"The Season of Learning"

Stage 1 - Learning about God

Lesson #1 - God, the Creator

The Bible (Scripture)

Then God said, "Let us make mankind in our image, in our likeness, so that they may rule over the fish in the sea and the birds in the sky, over the livestock and all the wild animals, and over all the creatures that move along the ground." So God created mankind in his own image, in the image of God he created them; male and female he created them. (Genesis 1:26-27 NIV)

A Prophetic Word

It is time to learn about our God. God is the creator of the universe. God in His infinite wisdom preserves the creation. God rules with authority and alone rules. Revealed to man in three persons, God shows us the father, the creator. As Son, God is preserver, righting all wrongs and bringing all things into order in turning over the creation to Jesus. Jesus, Christ our Lord, the ruler of all things. God has also revealed the Holy Spirit to preserve all things.

Self-Reflection

Have you experienced God? Do you trust your life (a creation) in the hands of God? Do you know that only God can build, repair and maintain the broken pieces of your life? Do you believe in God, the only one who can rebuild your broken pieces into an even greater masterpiece? Believe that God is your creator.

Adult Journal (Share your thoughts)

_____

_____

_____

_____

_____

_____

_____

_____

A Prophetic Point

God is the master builder and restorer of your life.

Poem

God, created the world, sun, moon and stars, Grass, flowers and trees
God put the ideas in our minds to create cars and boats that sail the seas

God created Sharks, turtles, flies and bumble bees
Things we like and things we don't, but God made them as He pleased

God created us and then created us to reign
To live within our purpose, we should operate the same

Men and women must rule
That's God's expectation
Created by God and called to
Rule Over the rest of creation

Caring for, protecting it,
Being responsible for them
Not destroying it,
But prolonging life that lives within

God created the creatures, but also the planet.
We live on it, and care for it. It's ours to manage.

Prayer

God create in us a heightened awareness of your presence

Lesson #2 - God's power

The Bible (Scripture)

God blessed them and said to them, "Be fruitful and increase in number; fill the earth and subdue it. Rule over the fish in the sea and the birds in the sky and over every living creature that moves on the ground." Then God said, "I give you every seed-bearing plant on the face of the whole earth and every tree that has fruit with seed in it. They will be yours for food. And to all the beasts of the earth and all the birds in the sky and all the creatures that move along the ground—everything that has the breath of life in it—I give every green plant for food." And it was so. God saw all that he had made, and it was very good. And there was evening, and there was morning—the sixth day. (Genesis 1:28-31 NIV)

A Prophetic Word

Men and women were created in God's image to be able to rule. We were blessed and designed to physically increase and subdue the earth. God saw all that he had made and it was very good. Just imagine, God created us in paradise, a heaven of sorts. Similarly, God has blessed us to live spiritually in the kingdom of God. We were created in God's image to share in God's authority. With this authority we are able to obey and exercise God's authority to conquer and rule. God has filled us with a spiritual heritage with gifts and power to love, overcome and conquer. Through this experience we get to learn of God's power & acts in creation.

What a mighty God we serve.

Self-Reflection

Consider placing your focus on God today. Only God is revealing Himself to you. God is also revealing His power that He has placed inside of you. These discoveries can change your life. What are you learning about God?

Adult Journal (Share your thoughts)

_____

_____

_____

_____

_____

_____

_____

_____

A Prophetic Point

Behold Him and be like Him. Be empowered!

Poem

Your God has power
God can do what he wants and He has the power carry it out

He created the world by His might
God has the past, present and future all at once in sight

God created people and the situations we live in
We need to know the God of our situations while we are in them.

Knowing God as creator means knowing who made me
Knowing who owns me, and who will step in and save me!

Here is a truth to savor.
He alone is our creator!

Prayer

God make us more like you. Share your spirit with us and let us learn to create opportunities to love like you.

Lesson #3 - God's Authority

The Bible (Scripture)

Let everyone be subject to the governing authorities, for there is no authority except that which God has established. The authorities that exist have been established by God. Consequently, whoever rebels against the authority is rebelling against what God has instituted, and those who do so will bring judgment on themselves. For rulers hold no terror for those who do right, but for those who do wrong. Do you want to be free from fear of the one in authority? Then do what is right and you will be commended. For the one in authority is God's servant for your good. But if you do wrong, be afraid, for rulers do not bear the sword for no reason. They are God's servants, agents of wrath to bring punishment on the wrongdoer. Therefore, it is necessary to submit to the authorities, not only because of possible punishment but also as a matter of conscience. (Romans 13:1-5 NIV)

A Prophetic Word

Family let us learn to succumb to those in charge, whether it is authority in the church, in the home, in the workplace or in the community. Our God created authority. God sets the standard for obedience. God requires obedience. God gives commands and makes decisions that are fulfilled by men. We become obedient because God says so. Only God has that right and that power.

God chose to give that right to His servants, who in turn oversee men everywhere in all walks of life. God's servants govern our activities, our growth and development. They make sure we achieve what God wants. God uses His authority to either bless or curse us. It all depends on whether or not we submit to God.

Self-Reflection

Will you abide by the authorities and laws of God or will you rebel against God and violate them? The blessing or curse is your choice!

Adult Journal (Share your thoughts)

_____

_____

_____

_____

_____

_____

A Prophetic Point

Treat God's laws as opportunities to be blessed.

Poem

Let us obey those that lead
For, it's really to God that we heed.

God appointed them,
God anointed them
God chose them, not us

There's nothing left to discuss.
They are an extension of our God,
Disobey! Rise up and fight, and your opponent will be God.

Recognize your God in whomever He uses
Surrender to your God and obey!
There are no excuses,
It's your love for God on display.

It is better to be showered by God's love,
What a horror it would be,
To be slaughtered by God's wrath
Because you don't recognize His authority!

Stage 2 - Knowing God

Lesson #4 - God the Father

The Bible (Scripture)

Since ancient times no one has heard, no ear has perceived, no eye has seen any God besides you, who acts on behalf of those who wait for him. You come to the help of those who gladly do right, who remember your ways. But when we continued to sin against them, you were angry. How then can we be saved? All of us have become like one who is unclean, and all our righteous acts are like filthy rags; we all shrivel up like a leaf, and like the wind our sins sweep us away. No one calls on your name or strives to lay hold of you; for you have hidden your face from us and have given us over to our sins. Yet you, LORD, are our Father. We are the clay, you are the potter; we are all the work of your hand. (Isaiah 64:4-9)

A Prophetic Word

You alone are God. You help us do right. You are our father, our great God. We are your people, your workmanship. You created us to love you and praise you, to connect to you and glorify you. We don't wait on you or chase after you. We don't long for you and seek you out to fill our hearts. Instead we sin against you and anger you. Though you allow us to wallow in sin for a season, you are the only one that can rescue us. Have mercy on us God. Remind us of your great power.

Self-Reflection

Why would man deny God and stray from the only one who can help? Look inward and find what you love and enjoy. Would searching for that cause you to forget about God? When you find the thing that makes you wander, call it out, confess it and recognize it. It will never sneak up on you again. Though it is valuable, it will keep you from pursing God. There is nothing greater than the Father!

Adult Journal (Share your thoughts)

_____

_____

_____

_____

_____

_____

_____

A Prophetic Point

Search for God again. He will help you.

Prayer

Lord, teach us to know you, and recognize your ways. Teach us to search for you with our hearts and desire to please you. Let us be shaped by you. Then we will belong to you. Amen

Lesson #5 - Holy Spirit

The Bible (Scripture)

When the day of Pentecost came, they were all together in one place. Suddenly a sound like the blowing of a violent wind came from heaven and filled the whole house where they were sitting. They saw what seemed to be tongues of fire that separated and came to rest on each of them. All of them were filled with the Holy Spirit and began to speak in other tongues as the Spirit enabled them. Now there were staying in Jerusalem God-fearing Jews from every nation under heaven. When they heard this sound, a crowd came together in bewilderment, because each one heard their own language being spoken. Utterly amazed, they asked: "Aren't all these who are speaking Galileans? Then how is it that each of us hears them in our native language? Parthians, Medes and Elamites; residents of Mesopotamia, Judea and Cappadocia, Pontus and Asia, Phrygia and Pamphylia, Egypt and the parts of Libya near Cyrene; visitors from Rome (both Jews and converts to Judaism); Cretans and Arabs—we hear them declaring the wonders of God in our own tongues!" Amazed and perplexed, they asked one another, "What does this mean?" Some, however, made fun of them and said, "They have had too much wine." (Acts 2:1-13 NIV)

A Prophetic Word

The believers were together. Tongues of fire rested on each of them. They were filled with the spirit and spoke through them in other languages declaring the wonders of God. The visitors (Jew and Gentile) wondered what this meant. I ask you what does this mean. For the disciples it meant they finally experienced the presence of the Comforter. They were used by God to declare His wonders. They were proof that it pays to wait on God. It also pays to wait together. For the visitors they watched a move of God up close. They too, had a close encounter with God.

Self-Reflection

Are you willing to be different? Are you ready to experience God? His spirit wants to live in and through you. Watch God at work in others' lives. Now watch God at work with you. Can you let the Holy Spirit move in and take control? Do you need to get out of the way? What is in you that could get in the way?

Adult Journal (Share your thoughts)

_____

_____

_____

_____

_____

_____

_____

A Prophetic Point

The Holy Spirit wants to move through you too!

Poem

Oh mighty wind of Pentecost,
We wait on you at great cost!

To be filled, with tongues of fire
Oh mighty wind take our spirits higher

To speak in words unknown to me, or in words unknown to all
Oh mighty it's time to fall!

Fall afresh on us oh wind,
Fall and let it have no end

Fall, we are on one accord
Make unto us a threefold chord

Oh mighty wind, Spirit of God,
Burn our flesh until it's charred

Oh mighty wind,
Our God that flies, purify, purify!
Oh mighty wind we wait for you.
We need your power, we need you!

Lesson #6 - The power of Christ

The Bible (Scripture)

Then Peter stood up with the Eleven, raised his voice and addressed the crowd: "Fellow Jews and all of you who live in Jerusalem, let me explain this to you; listen carefully to what I say. These people are not drunk, as you suppose. It's only nine in the morning! No, this is what was spoken by the prophet Joel: 'In the last days, God says, I will pour out my Spirit on all people. Your sons and daughters will prophesy, your young men will see visions, your old men will dream dreams. Even on my servants, both men and women, I will pour out my Spirit in those days, and they will prophesy. I will show wonders in the heavens above and signs on the earth below, blood and fire and billows of smoke. The sun will be turned to darkness and the moon to blood before the coming of the great and glorious day of the Lord. And everyone who calls on the name of the Lord will be saved.' (Acts 2:14-21 NIV)

A Prophetic Word

This is a crucial time now. God is speaking through His spirit. God is communicating through man and woman. He is prophesying, dreaming, having visions, revealing heavenly wonders and using earthly signs. God is showing you unbelievable things in Heavenly objects. They are here to show you the times to let you know we are closer to the return of the Lord Jesus Christ.

Self-Reflection

God's power will change you. Ask for His power to now! Proclaim the change you want.

Adult Journal (Share your thoughts)

_____

_____

_____

_____

_____

_____

_____

A Prophetic Point

Prepare your hearts to receive the spirit and be saved!

Prayer

Lord, pour out your Spirit on us. Let us see your word, hear your word and feel your presence. Give us the power to proclaim your word to the whole world. Give us the strength to share the message that Jesus Christ was crucified for our sins and that men can believe in Him and be saved!

Stage 3 - God's Salvation

Lesson #7 - The Crucifixion I

The Bible (Scripture)

As they were going out, they met a man from Cyrene, named Simon, and they forced him to carry the cross. They came to a place called Golgotha (which means "the place of the skull"). There they offered Jesus wine to drink, mixed with gall; but after tasting it, he refused to drink it. When they had crucified him, they divided up his clothes by casting lots. And sitting down, they kept watch over him there. Above his head they placed the written charge against him: This is Jesus, The King of the Jews. (Matthew 27:32-38 NIV)

A Prophetic Word

Golgotha, represents and symbolizes the world's fixation with death and destruction. It's also the site of the master's cross, which represents our redemption. On the cross, at Golgotha, Jesus tasted the mixture of wine and gall but failed to drink it. On the contrary, he drank from the cup of suffering. He endured pain and humiliation for our sakes. Jesus tasted death for us. While he suffered, they gambled for his clothes. They mocked his name. If only they knew Jesus' crucifixion was for their salvation.

Self-Reflection

What does His sacrifice mean to you? If Jesus' sacrifice means anything to you, then make a sacrifice to him. Whatever Jesus calls you to do, obey Him.

Adult Journal (Share your thoughts)

_____

_____

_____

_____

_____

_____

_____

A Prophetic Point

The cross revealed the truth in Jesus! You will bear a cross that will reveal the truth in you!

Prayer

Lord, every time we see the cross, remind us that it requires a lifetime of faithful love and service in honor of Jesus and obedience to the will of God. Amen!

Lesson #8 - The Crucifixion II

The Bible (Scripture)

Two rebels were crucified with him, one on his right and one on his left. Those who passed by hurled insults at him, shaking their heads and saying, "You who are going to destroy the temple and build it in three days, save yourself! Come down from the cross, if you are the Son of God!" In the same way the chief priests, the teachers of the law and the elders mocked him. "He saved others," they said, "but he can't save himself! He's the king of Israel! Let him come down now from the cross, and we will believe in him. He trusts in God. Let God rescue him now if he wants him, for he said, 'I am the Son of God.'" In the same way the rebels who were crucified with him also heaped insults on him. (Matthew 27:38-44 NIV)

A Prophetic Word

How horrid when you are going through and people that are with you crucify you too. It's enough that you are going through. It's worse when others see it and mistreat you. Jesus went through this. Jesus suffered mistaken identity. He was mistaken for a criminal. He was accused of being reckless and accused of threatening to destroy the temple. This is the chief cornerstone of the church. He was tempted and mocked, and told to trust God. The Son of God, the savior of man turned His persecutors into believers.

Self-Reflection

When no one believes in you, your God or what your God is going to do in your life, just remember they didn't believe in Jesus either. Even if others don't see it, will you trust that a change is taking place in you? Reflect on your life and the change that is taking place. Remind yourself that it started with Jesus' outstretched arms on the cross.

Adult Journal (Share your thoughts)

_____

_____

_____

_____

_____

_____

_____

A Prophetic Point

When you have to go it alone for a season, you will survive if you simply trust in God!

Poem

Two men crucified,
One on each side

No one believes or trusts God.
There is no faith!
No one loves God
Only insults, just hate!

He endured hammers, nails, blood and death,
Taking His very last breath

He suffered knowing we didn't believe in Him,
Yet he saved us from our sins!

On the cross!

Lesson #9 - The Crucifixion III

The Bible (Scripture)

From noon until three in the afternoon darkness came over all the land. About three in the afternoon Jesus cried out in a loud voice, *"Eli, Eli, lema sabachthani?"* (Which means "My God, my God, why have you forsaken me?").When some of those standing there heard this, they said, "He's calling Elijah." Immediately one of them ran and got a sponge. He filled it with wine vinegar, put it on a staff, and offered it to Jesus to drink. The rest said, "Now leave him alone. Let's see if Elijah comes to save him." And when Jesus had cried out again in a loud voice, he gave up his spirit. At that moment the curtain of the temple was torn in two from top to bottom. The earth shook, the rocks split and the tombs broke open. The bodies of many holy people who had died were raised to life. They came out of the tombs after Jesus' resurrection and went into the holy city and appeared to many people. When the centurion and those with him who were guarding Jesus saw the earthquake and all that had happened, they were terrified, and exclaimed, "Surely he was the Son of God!" Many women were there, watching from a distance. They had followed Jesus from Galilee to care for his needs. (Matthew 27:45-55 NIV)

A Prophetic Word

The crucifixion was epic, featuring a dying savior in a darkened land, crying out in faith, for a heavenly father that cannot watch the sins that Jesus bore (took on) for us. It also featured the parting of the Holy Spirit, who would later return to resurrect Jesus from the grave. Through the death of Jesus the Christ, the Holy Spirit later became available to all believers, to resurrect us from a life of sin to a spirit filled life.

When Jesus was crucified, the curtain of the temple was torn. The presence of God was made available to us all. The tombs were opened, and the dead were raised.

Self-Reflection

God wants to move in your life and reveal more of Himself to you. What area of your life will be raised and renewed? Are there hopes, dreams, or relationships waiting? Is there a sense of identity, or belonging that was destroyed?

Adult Journal (Share your thoughts)

_____

_____

_____

_____

_____

_____

A Prophetic Point

It is time for renewal!

Prayer

Lord, let us learn to trust in you
We suffer when we're going through

Lord, let the spirit lead us to
The destination designed by you

That's what Jesus died to do
Share His spirit, comfort too

The curtain was torn in two
So that we may come to you

Bodies rose, Jesus rose
We will rise, now we know

We'll walk the step, of the master
He said greater will come after

Greater things we will do
But the Spirit makes lives brand new

We will help win the lost
Because there is power in the cross

<u>Lesson #10 – Faith</u>

The Bible (Scripture)

While he was saying this, a synagogue leader came and knelt before him and said, "My daughter has just died. But come and put your hand on her, and she will live." Jesus got up and went with him, and so did his disciples. Just then a woman who had been subject to bleeding for twelve years came up behind him and touched the edge of his cloak. She said to herself, "If I only touch his cloak, I will be healed." Jesus turned and saw her. "Take heart, daughter," he said, "your faith has healed you." And the woman was healed at that moment. When Jesus entered the synagogue leader's house and saw the noisy crowd and people playing pipes, he said, "Go away. The girl is not dead but asleep." But they laughed at him. After the crowd had been put outside, he went in and took the girl by the hand, and she got up. News of this spread through all that region. (Matthew 9:18-26 NIV)

A Prophetic Word

At a man's request, Jesus went to go touch the young girl and bring her back to life. Meanwhile, a woman touched Jesus and received her own healing, thus restoring her own quality of life. Jesus acknowledged the woman's faith brought her healing. It was understood that the man's faith restored his daughter.

It's amazing what our faith in Jesus can do. If God can do anything, and we can believe in him to do what we need, then we can certainly experience it for ourselves. What's even more amazing is that if we can believe it, we often have to act on what we believe. It may be a touch. Find your moment to reach out and touch Jesus. All it takes is a prayer. Ask Jesus to touch you. He will do it.

Self-Reflection

What do you need from God to make your life whole, and balanced? Don't be dismayed.

Adult Journal (Share your thoughts)

_____

_____

_____

_____

_____

_____

A Prophetic Point

God can and will do anything for you. Just ask!

Prayer

Lord teach us to see the impossible, to remember that we can do it and believe that we will do it.

Lesson #11 – Forgiveness

The Bible (Scripture)

Then Peter came to Jesus and asked, "Lord, how many times shall I forgive my brother or sister who sins against me? Up to seven times?" Jesus answered, "I tell you, not seven times, but seventy-seven times. "Therefore, the kingdom of heaven is like a king who wanted to settle accounts with his servants. As he began the settlement, a man who owed him ten thousand bags of gold was brought to him. Since he was not able to pay, the master ordered that he and his wife and his children and all that he had be sold to repay the debt.

"At this the servant fell on his knees before him. 'Be patient with me,' he begged, 'and I will pay back everything.' The servant's master took pity on him, canceled the debt and let him go. "But when that servant went out, he found one of his fellow servants who owed him a hundred silver coins. He grabbed him and began to choke him. 'Pay back what you owe me!' he demanded. "His fellow servant fell to his knees and begged him, 'Be patient with me, and I will pay it back.' "But he refused. Instead, he went off and had the man thrown into prison until he could pay the debt. When the other servants saw what had happened, they were outraged and went and told their master everything that had happened. "Then the master called the servant in. 'You wicked servant,' he said, 'I canceled all that debt of yours because you begged me to. Shouldn't you have had mercy on your fellow servant just as I had on you?' In anger his master handed him over to the jailers to be tortured, until he should pay back all he owed. (Matthew 18:21-34 NIV)

A Prophetic Word

No matter how many times you have been wronged, you cannot forgive your friend enough. Your heart is never large enough, sincere enough, forgiving enough to outlast the things that will offend you.

You are never close enough to the pure wellspring of life to remain in a state of perfect peace. You may rarely fall to intentional sin, but you will definitely be challenged by friendly fire. In other words, you will experience the hurt and pain from being in relationship with others. It is sometimes enough to cause you to retreat or wander into a place of sin. It many cases, it can drive you to search for Jesus for the strength to continue on.

The nature of collateral relationships is that they drive us to seek another relationship to strengthen us to and help us withstand more. Wrong doing from others nudges us to Jesus Christ for the ability to forgive. Only in the surrendering to God for, can we submit ourselves to each other in love.

A Prophetic Point

Continue in humility, approach God with reverence.

Self-Reflection

Are you willing to forgive others and continue on in loving relationships with them? If so, are you willing to commit your heart to God even more, so you are equipped to forgive them when needed?

Adult Journal (Share your thoughts)

_____

_____

_____

_____

_____

Poem

We wrestle with these questions,

Though we know the truth

Our daily encounters become routine lessons,

And the answers become absolutes.

Etched in our hearts after the hundredth time

That we fail to forgive, we are stuck on rewind.

Should we forgive? Can we forgive? Why should I forgive him or her?

How often should I forgive? How many times should I forgive someone that

does not deserve?

For, if God forgives, you should forgive!

If you don't, then He won't either.

Expect an endless cycle of pain, you will never get a breather!

If you forgive, then God will lift the weight off of your heart

The little bit of hate you held was tearing your apart.

Forgiveness builds relationships, forgiving is demanding

You start out with an acquaintanceship that takes flight and comes down for a

landing.

Your status as friends is up in the air, then when you are forced to forgive

You begin to invest in a person, and your relationship begins to live.

Forgiveness is hard work, it's very difficult at times.

It makes you faithful, sincere, holy down inside.

Who can have a patient heart that forgives man's frequent wrongs?

That's the one who forgives and quietly lives right with God?

Stage 4 - Life in God's Church

Lesson #12 - The Church

The Bible (Scripture)

They devoted themselves to the apostles' teaching and to fellowship, to the breaking of bread and to prayer. Everyone was filled with awe at the many wonders and signs performed by the apostles. All the believers were together and had everything in common. They sold property and possessions to give to anyone who had need. Every day they continued to meet together in the temple courts. They broke bread in their homes and ate together with glad and sincere hearts, praising God and enjoying the favor of all the people. And the Lord added to their number daily those who were being saved. (Acts 2:42-47 NIV)

A Prophetic Word

There is nothing like God's church. The world offers pursuits that lead to nowhere, vices that leave you with nothing, pleasures that rob you and leave you broken and pride that strips you and knocks you down. The church however, offers an alternative. Well, the church offers life. For the believer, the church awakens you to the wonders of God where through faith in Jesus we commit ourselves to the family of believers. Faithful teaching instructs us, fellowship keeps us, and prayer strengthens us. We watch God move through visible signs and wonders. Together we are on one accord, our hearts touched, filled with praise, our spirits set ablaze with love by the fire of the Holy Spirit.

Self-Reflection

Do you go to church? Are you a member of one? Are you willing to live, truly live? The church is the body of

Christ. If you visit it a little, you will experience a little. If you dedicate your life to it, you will find life in it. In the church, we help each other, inspire each other and sacrifice for each other, so that we are all grafted in, together. We share fellowship with one another in the church. Ask yourself if you are ready.

Adult Journal (Share your thoughts)

_____

_____

_____

_____

_____

_____

A Prophetic Point

Get it together. Get in the spirit with the rest of the church and enjoy the life that is waiting for you!

Poem

There's life and death

That we must choose

There's hope or sorrow

For us to use

Sickness and pain lie in wait

But faith is waiting to determine our fate

Opposing forces all at work

You should choose to join the church

Or choose the world, and all its cares

Manipulated by the prince of air

Who lurks and searches for men to tempt

You and I are not exempt

Evil waits and works in men

To tease and please and draw you in

But there is help that will suffice

There's power in the body of Christ.

Join the church of God today

The kingdom awaits Christ is the way!

Lesson #13 - Baptism

The Bible (Scripture)

Then Jesus came from Galilee to the Jordan to be baptized by John. But John tried to deter him, saying, "I need to be baptized by you, and do you come to me?" Jesus replied, "Let it be so now; it is proper for us to do this to fulfill all righteousness." Then John consented. As soon as Jesus was baptized, he went up out of the water. At that moment heaven was opened, and he saw the Spirit of God descending like a dove and alighting on him. And a voice from heaven said, "This is my Son, whom I love; with him I am well pleased." (Matthew 3:13-17 NIV)

A Prophetic Word

Jesus was with us but separate from us. When Jesus approached John to be baptized, John appeared to hesitate. He told Jesus "I need to be baptized by you." Jesus responded, "Let it be so now." That is a word we all need to comfort us.

As we rush through life in this digital, multimedia, multitasking, quick fix, readymade age of expediency. We are faced with God's correction. Since we cannot race God to get to our next blessing, we are faced with the challenge of slowing down. We have to walk at God's pace, wait for God's timing, get into God's flow and enjoy God's atmosphere. As God takes us higher into deeper spiritual realms, we have to develop a sense of awareness, appreciation and reverence for where we are, and for what God is doing in our lives. The Father led Jesus to be baptized. He would then lead Jesus into public ministry, through trials and onto glory

Self-Reflection

Do you recognize the privilege bestowed upon you? Do you know that God is with you, leading you somewhere? Are you willing to slow down and develop presence a stronger sense of presence by recognizing God's presence, acknowledging that God is with you?

Adult Journal (Share your thoughts)

Baptism is when you tell the world that you have died to a life of sin and that you have been resurrected with Christ. What have you done to tell others that you live for Christ now? Who have you told? What ways can you think of to show others that you are grateful for Jesus and love Him?

_____

_____

_____

_____

_____

_____

A Prophetic Point

Slow down and be present with God. Acknowledging how God is developing your spirit.
Acknowledge what God is doing in your life.

Prayer

Father, teach us to follow the Lord Jesus, to obey your commands, surrender to your will, to fulfill your plan As we are baptized into the faith, through grace, Let all heaven and earth witness as we take a stand for Christ.

Lesson #14 - Last Supper

The Bible (Scripture)

On the first day of the Festival of Unleavened Bread, the disciples came to Jesus and asked, "Where do you want us to make preparations for you to eat the Passover?" 18 He replied, "Go into the city to a certain man and tell him, 'The Teacher says: My appointed time is near. I am going to celebrate the Passover with my disciples at your house.'" 19 So the disciples did as Jesus had directed them and prepared the Passover. 20 When evening came, Jesus was reclining at the table with the Twelve. (Matthew 26:17-20 NIV)

While they were eating, Jesus took bread, and when he had given thanks, he broke it and gave it to his disciples, saying, "Take and eat; this is my body." Then he took a cup, and when he had given thanks, he gave it to them, saying, "Drink from it, all of you. 28 This is my blood of the covenant, which is poured out for many for the forgiveness of sins. 29 I tell you, I will not drink from this fruit of the vine from now on until that day when I drink it new with you in my Father's kingdom." 30 When they had sung a hymn, they went out to the Mount of Olives. (Matthew 26:26-30 NIV)

A Prophetic Word

Jesus introduced the disciples to the Last Supper. They drank from the cup, which represented the blood of the covenant. They probably didn't know a thing about the covenant that Jesus was establishing with them. They would not have known why they were drinking the cup. Nor would they have been able to grasp the concept of juice representing Jesus' blood.

They were enjoying the Last Supper but were clueless about it. Later they could look back on this moment of fellowship and make the connection between Jesus' death on the cross and their commemorating (preparing) for it with Jesus at the table. Still today, we gather together celebrating Jesus' death on the cross. It is the sacrifice of His body and blood. We remember Jesus' act of obedience. Our faith in His suffering, death and resurrection is the bond that unites us. The bible teaches us to forsake not the gathering of the saints.

Self-Reflection

I challenge you to commit to the Lord's Supper and remember the sacrifice, and remember the extension of grace you've received from God. Not only has God forgiven you of your sins, but what are the consequences of sin, God has exempted you from.

Adult Journal (Share your thoughts)

_____

_____

_____

_____

_____

_____

_____

A Prophetic Point

God has given you a divine moment to remember Him. Join the congregation and count your blessings!

Poem

When it's time to regenerate,

Time to let our spirits rise

For refreshing, and refocus on Christ alone

Our king sits enthroned

With glory and compassion to share

His love, Embroidered on our hearts, living there

We come to worship, leave to serve

Obeying, and we live unnerved

With steps divinely ordered above

We walk in the power of Jesus' blood

Then we return to resume our place

Before the throne, receiving grace

Let praise resound, as we sing

The body of the risen King!

Lesson #15 - Last Supper II

The Bible (Scripture)

And while they were eating, he said, "Truly I tell you, one of you will betray me." [22] They were very sad and began to say to him one after the other, "Surely you don't mean me, Lord?" [23] Jesus replied, "The one who has dipped his hand into the bowl with me will betray me. [24] The Son of Man will go just as it is written about him. But woe to that man who betrays the Son of Man! It would be better for him if he had not been born." [25] Then Judas, the one who would betray him, said, "Surely you don't mean me, Rabbi?" Jesus answered, "You have said so." (Matthew 26:21-25 NIV)

A Prophetic Word

This excerpt of the story of the Lord's Supper is about betrayal versus commitment. The disciples were not aware of their spiritual propensity to sin. Jesus explained that one of the disciples would betray Him. It would only occur because this betrayal was a part of God's plan. Likewise, the persecution that Jesus would face and His ultimate death on the cross was ordained, prophesied, written, and was definitely going to happen.

Judas was compelled to betray the Lord. His heart was filled with sin, drawn by the temptation to reveal the Lord's location and moment of vulnerability to the enemy for money. Judas was morally corrupt and unfaithful to the Lord, but you and I can live committed to the Lord!

Self-Reflection

What has God planned for you and how can you ensure your life pleases God?

Adult Journal (Share your thoughts)

_____

_____

_____

_____

_____

_____

_____

A Prophetic Point

As you remember His sacrifice, He will awaken you!

Prayer

Lord, preserve us for your salvation Let us unite in fellowship together, in suffering together, in service together, in persecution, in spiritual training and spiritual war together. Keep us from falling. Keep us near you.

Stage 5 - God's Scripture

Lesson #16 - Sacred Scripture I

The Bible (Scripture)

Then Jesus was led by the Spirit into the wilderness to be tempted by the devil. After fasting forty days and forty nights, he was hungry. The tempter came to him and said, "If you are the Son of God, tell these stones to become bread." Jesus answered, "It is written: 'Man shall not live on bread alone, but on every word that comes from the mouth of God.'" (Matthew 4:1-4 NIV)

A Prophetic Word

Jesus' defense against the devil was the word of God. There was no sinful desire that had Him; therefore there was no temptation that could not seize Him. Jesus hid the scriptures in His heart. The truth of the scripture reminded Jesus of who He was and how to live. They led to righteous living. Many of us behold selfish desires, greed, and ambition, which leave us susceptible to temptation and utter destruction. I challenge you to be filled with the word of God, to maintain the knowledge of God, and to avoid, "every kind of wickedness, evil, greed and depravity. (Romans 1:29a NIV)

Self-Reflection

What are you filled with? What does it cause you to do? What does it protect you from?

Adult Journal (Share your thoughts)

_____

_____

_____

_____

_____

_____

_____

_____

_____

_____

A Prophetic Point

The Word has overcome the world. Get it in you before the world destroys you!

Prayer

Lord, our prayer is to be led by your word. Let our lives be directed by the light of your word, so we can live according to it. Strengthen us and preserve us according to every promise written in your word. Let your Holy name be praised!

Lesson #17 - Sacred Scripture II

The Bible (Scripture)

Then the devil took him to the holy city and had him stand on the highest point of the temple. "If you are the Son of God," he said, "throw yourself down. For it is written: 'He will command his angels concerning you, and they will lift you up in their hands, so that you will not strike your foot against a stone.'" Jesus answered him, "It is also written: 'Do not put the Lord your God to the test.'" Again, the devil took him to a very high mountain and showed him all the kingdoms of the world and their splendor. "All this I will give you," he said, "if you will bow down and worship me." Jesus said to him, "Away from me, Satan! For it is written: 'Worship the Lord your God, and serve him only.'" Then the devil left him, and angels came and attended him. (Matthew 4:5-11 NIV)

A Prophetic Word

You will face situations that require you to use the word of God as your defense. You must also use the word as your offensive weapon of choice to fight. You will have to fight. In this world, you will face situations with people and things that will require you to fight spiritually. You "have divine power to demolish, arguments and every pretension that sets itself up against the knowledge of God."

Self-Reflection

I challenge you to match your power with the word of God.

Adult Journal (Share your thoughts)

_____

_____

_____

_____

_____

_____

A Prophetic Point

God will send help. Until then, help yourself to the Word and survive!

Prayer

God, reveal the treasure in your holy word. Sensitize me to keep it in my heart. I want to remember, and obey your holy word. Bless me according to your perfect word. I want to be like Jesus. I want to know your word, see the truth in your word, and place my faith and hope in it so I am rewarded by it. For, your word will forever show me the way. Help me to understand what's right according to your word and I will forever praise your Holy name. Amen!

Part II - Personal relationship with God

"The Season of Doing"

Stage 6 - Walking in Grace

Lesson #18 - Growing in grace

The Bible (Scripture)

Every year Jesus' parents went to Jerusalem for the Festival of the Passover. When he was twelve years old, they went up to the festival, according to the custom. After the festival was over, while his parents were returning home, the boy Jesus stayed behind in Jerusalem, but they were unaware of it. Thinking he was in their company, they traveled on for a day. Then they began looking for him among their relatives and friends. When they did not find him, they went back to Jerusalem to look for him. After three days they found him in the temple courts, sitting among the teachers, listening to them and asking them questions. Everyone who heard him was amazed at his understanding and his answers. When his parents saw him, they were astonished. His mother said to him, "Son, why have you treated us like this? Your father and I have been anxiously searching for you." "Why were you searching for me?" he asked. "Didn't you know I had to be in my Father's house?" But they did not understand what he was saying to them. Then he went down to Nazareth with them and was obedient to them. But his mother treasured all these things in her heart. And Jesus grew in wisdom and stature, and in favor with God and man. (Luke 2:41-52 NIV)

A Prophetic Word

There is a season in your life where you will be drawn to the church, drawn to listen and learn, to question and wrestle with the truths of God's scripture. Some will look for you, long for your company, remember the days of old with you. They will be looking for the old you, the comfortable you, that falls in line, and is there when you when they want you. You however, are called to a season of walking with the Father, learning His voice, and learning obedience.

Self-Reflection

Do you find yourself wanting to learn more about your God? Are you more sensitive to the presence of God? God may be calling you cancel your plans and remain in the overflow of God's spirit in some area of your life. Spend time in in God's presence, reading and praying. As you leave your time of devotions, don't forget God. Keep in mind what God shows you in His word. Remember what God speaks to your heart.

Adult Journal (Share your thoughts)

_____

_____

_____

_____

_____

_____

_____

A Prophetic Point

Walk in the grace that God gives you.

Lesson #19 - Compassion for others

The Bible (Scripture)

When Jesus heard what had happened, he withdrew by boat privately to a solitary place. Hearing of this, the crowds followed him on foot from the towns. When Jesus landed and saw a large crowd, he had compassion on them and healed their sick. As evening approached, the disciples came to him and said, "This is a remote place, and it's already getting late. Send the crowds away, so they can go to the villages and buy themselves some food." Jesus replied, "They do not need to go away. You give them something to eat." "We have here only five loaves of bread and two fish," they answered. "Bring them here to me," he said. And he directed the people to sit down on the grass. Taking the five loaves and the two fish and looking up to heaven, he gave thanks and broke the loaves. Then he gave them to the disciples, and the disciples gave them to the people. They all ate and were satisfied, and the disciples picked up twelve basketfuls of broken pieces that were left over. The number of those who ate was about five thousand men, besides women and children. (Matthew 14:13-21 NIV)

A Prophetic Word

Jesus went looking for a solitary place but was surrounded by a crowd that had followed Him. Jesus noticed the sick among them and out of compassion, He healed their sick. That's what happens when you are in relationship with God. God show compassion for those who fear Him. He notices those who follow Him, long to hear from Him and want to be touched by His loving kindness. God is aware of whatever you are going through. God is not interrupted by your needs. In fact, God schedules visitations with us and He accepts walk-ins at any time.

Self-Reflection

Find the time to communicate to God what you need. This walk in grace is a treasure to both you and God.

Adult Journal (Share your thoughts)

_____

_____

_____

_____

_____

_____

_____

_____

_____

_____

A Prophetic Point

God welcomes your company

Value every moment in His presence

Stage 7 - Daily Deliverance

Lesson #20 - Liberation

The Bible (Scripture)

But now, this is what the LORD says he who created you, Jacob, he who formed you, Israel: "Do not fear, for I have redeemed you; I have summoned you by name; you are mine. When you pass through the waters, I will be with you; and when you pass through the rivers, they will not sweep over you. When you walk through the fire, you will not be burned; the flames will not set you ablaze. For I am the LORD your God, the Holy One of Israel, your Savior; I give Egypt for your ransom, Cush and Seba in your stead. Since you are precious and honored in my sight, and because I love you, I will give people in exchange for you, nations in exchange for your life. Do not be afraid, for I am with you; I will bring your children from the east and gather you from the west. I will say to the north, 'Give them up!' and to the south, 'Do not hold them back.' Bring my sons from afar and my daughters from the ends of the earth - everyone who is called by my name, whom I created for my glory, whom I formed and made." (Isaiah 43:1-7 NIV)

A Prophetic Word

One of the great assets in life is the gift of knowing who you are and who you belong to. When you know that you belong to God, you will soon learn that God will protect you. God will not allow anyone or anything else to own or destroy you.

Know that God has chosen you. Know that God has called you to journey with Him. He knows your name. He knows the plans He has for you. In fact, He has a customized plan for you that will bless you tremendously.

Knowing all of this, you must learn and then expect trouble to come. When it comes, know that God is with you before the trouble comes. God is with you while the trouble is working against you, and God will be with you, when the trouble subsides. He will not let it consume you. Trouble will come at you in one area of your life; meanwhile, God will bless you in another area of life. Regardless of whatever is happening to you, God will show and prove that He loves you. God's revelation of love, and care for you will overrule anything that comes against you.

Self-Reflection

If you know that God is with you, and that God will never leave you or forsake you, then why do you stop believing it? Why do you allow yourself to doubt it? When God has been silent in your life, hasn't God shown up later? Doesn't God reward you for having faith?

Adult Journal (Share your thoughts)

_____

_____

_____

_____

_____

_____

_____

A Prophetic Point

You belong to God.

Now Belong!

Lesson #21 – Rescued

The Bible (Scripture)

So the king gave the order, and they brought Daniel and threw him into the lions' den. The king said to Daniel, "May your God, whom you serve continually, rescue you!" A stone was brought and placed over the mouth of the den, and the king sealed it with his own signet ring and with the rings of his nobles, so that Daniel's situation might not be changed. Then the king returned to his palace and spent the night without eating and without any entertainment being brought to him. And he could not sleep. At the first light of dawn, the king got up and hurried to the lions' den. When he came near the den, he called to Daniel in an anguished voice, "Daniel, servant of the living God, has your God, whom you serve continually, been able to rescue you from the lions?" Daniel answered, "May the king live forever! My God sent his angel, and he shut the mouths of the lions. They have not hurt me, because I was found innocent in his sight. Nor have I ever done any wrong before you, Your Majesty." The king was overjoyed and gave orders to lift Daniel out of the den. And when Daniel was lifted from the den, no wound was found on him, because he had trusted in his God. At the king's command, the men who had falsely accused Daniel were brought in and thrown into the lions' den, along with their wives and children. And before they reached the floor of the den, the lions overpowered them and crushed all their bones. (Daniel 6:16-24 NIV)

A Prophetic Word

When Daniel was thrown into the Lion's Den, the king said to Daniel, "May your God, whom you serve continually, rescue you!" There is an eternal truth hidden here. It is that your God whom you serve continually, will rescue you! He most certainly will.

Like Daniel, your situation might not change. You may have to fast and pray, or you may have someone fast and pray with you or for you. Regardless, there are times when you will go through the situation. God may not deliver from that situation. He may not remove that situation, but rest assure that God will deliver you while you are in that situation.

God may do it in divine fashion, by restricting your enemy, by placing a hedge of protection around you, by divine miracle that can't be explained. God may use people, places and things, to block the attack on you. God may answer your prayer, or the collective prayers of the righteous. God may have mercy on you at the last minute and spare you. God may have planned all along to allow this situation, knowing it would challenge your faith. Perhaps, God orchestrated the situation to reveal your faith to others. Either way, God allows it. God is with you in it and God will secure you from the danger in your present situation.

Self-Reflection

Do you believe in God? In difficult times, do you believe that God wants to bring you out? Do you believe that God will step in before your suffering is too much to bear? Do you believe that God wants you to live and overcome all obstacles? Do you believe that God has a positive outcome for you? If not, then believe. God wants to help you realize that all of this is true. God wants to deliver you!

Adult Journal (Share your thoughts)

_____

_____

_____

_____

_____

_____

_____

_____

_____

_____

<u>A Prophetic Point</u>

As you pack for the journey, plan for tough battles. You will win some and lose some. Regardless of the outcome, if you have faith, God wins!

Lesson #22 - Saved for others' sake

The Bible (Scripture)

Then King Darius wrote to all the nations and peoples of every language in all the earth: "May you prosper greatly! "I issue a decree that in every part of my kingdom people must fear and reverence the God of Daniel. "For he is the living God and he endures forever; his kingdom will not be destroyed, his dominion will never end. He rescues and he saves; he performs signs and wonders in the heavens and on the earth. He has rescued Daniel from the power of the lions." So Daniel prospered during the reign of Darius and the reign of Cyrus the Persian. (Daniel 6:35-38)

A Prophetic Word

The bible says that we are born twice, once of our mother and then from God. We are also twice called, called from the darkness to the marvelous light, which is for us a call to come home, to God. God calls us to live here on earth in God's presence where we walk and talk with God, and then God calls us home to live in eternity with Him in glory (heaven). While we are here, God reveals to us the redemptive work done on the cross by Jesus Christ. Then God calls us to follow Jesus. Though Jesus no longer walks on the earth, His presence is still felt and followed. We join the church and follow His leading and promptings in the spirit. We enter into trials. We are delivered from them. Our faith increases with each one. Our passion grows with each one.

It is always marvelous to see faith grown in others when our faith is tested and revealed. Someone as we suffer, others grow. King Darius issued a decree that people must fear and reverence the God of Daniel, the living God that endures forever. While the king's decree could only invoke an outward demonstration of reverence, we know that an internal, indwelling fear of God would only come by way of experience. Nevertheless, King Daniel recognized that God rescues and he saves, performs signs and wonders in the heavens and on the earth, and is worthy of our praise.

Self-Reflection

Acknowledge these truths about our God and do likewise.

Adult Journal (Share your thoughts)

_____

_____

_____

_____

_____

_____

_____

A Prophetic Point

Be faithful to God. It is proof that God is alive!

Lesson #23 - "Restored"

The Bible (Scripture)

Early in the morning, Jesus stood on the shore, but the disciples did not realize that it was Jesus. He called out to them, "Friends, haven't you any fish?" "No," they answered. He said, "Throw your net on the right side of the boat and you will find some." When they did, they were unable to haul the net in because of the large number of fish. Then the disciple whom Jesus loved said to Peter, "It is the Lord!" As soon as Simon Peter heard him say, "It is the Lord," he wrapped his outer garment around him (for he had taken it off) and jumped into the water. The other disciples followed in the boat, towing the net full of fish, for they were not far from shore, about a hundred yards. When they landed, they saw a fire of burning coals there with fish on it, and some bread. Jesus said to them, "Bring some of the fish you have just caught." So Simon Peter climbed back into the boat and dragged the net ashore. It was full of large fish, 153, but even with so many the net was not torn. Jesus said to them, "Come and have breakfast." None of the disciples dared ask him, "Who are you?" They knew it was the Lord. Jesus came, took the bread and gave it to them, and did the same with the fish. This was now the third time Jesus appeared to his disciples after he was raised from the dead. (John 21:1-14 NIV)

A Prophetic Word

The disciples were once again fishing with no success. Jesus had mercy on them and guided them. They obeyed and caught more fish than they could handle. Then Jesus told them to bring some of the fish and they shared a private moment of fellowship with them.

For Peter, this was restoration as he had recently betrayed Jesus and fallen away. For the rest of the disciples, this was also restorative, if you can recall, they were all scattered, running away in fear when Jesus was arrested. For all of the disciples, this was empowering. Jesus gave them proof that He had risen. He inspired them to continue on in the faith. Jesus showed them that obedience still worked even after suffered death on the cross at the hands of the Roman soldiers. For the rest of us this is further proof that God forgives; God restores; God honors obedience; God still has plans for us when broken and when whole. Jesus overcame the grave so that we too can become overcomers.

Self-Reflection

I challenge you to examine yourself. Find where your relationships are broken. Find where your faith in God is broken. Find where you are hurting and need healing, then ask God to restore you. As you walk with the Lord, you will suffer. You will bend, even break. You will be healed! When the Lord restores his people, let Jacob rejoice and Israel be glad! (Psalm 14:7b)

Adult Journal (Share your thoughts)

_____

_____

_____

_____

_____

_____

_____

_____

_____

A Prophetic Point

When you have the chance to restore your relationship with Jesus, leave everything behind and go for it!

Stage 8 - Developing Discipline

Lesson #24 - "Fasting & Prayer"

The Bible (Scripture)

And when you pray, do not be like the hypocrites, for they love to pray standing in the synagogues and on the street corners to be seen by others. Truly I tell you, they have received their reward in full. But when you pray, go into your room, close the door and pray to your Father, who is unseen. Then your Father, who sees what is done in secret, will reward you. And when you pray, do not keep on babbling like pagans, for they think they will be heard because of their many words. Do not be like them, for your Father knows what you need before you ask him. "This, then, is how you should pray: "'Our Father in heaven, hallowed be your name, your kingdom come, your will be done, on earth as it is in heaven. Give us today our daily bread. And forgive us our debts, as we also have forgiven our debtors. And lead us not into temptation, but deliver us from the evil one.' (Matthew 6:5-13 NIV)

A Prophetic Word

Spiritual growth requires discipline. Developing discipline involves fasting and prayer. Jesus taught the disciples that prayer requires faith. It is best demonstrated in private between you and God. God knows what you need. God has no problem blessing you with your needs and God wants you to demonstrate your faith to God. That pleases God. A sincere life pleases God, and prayer from a sincere heart is honored. God wants you groomed and polished for His presence. God wants you surrendered to the prayer answerer before you seek answered prayers. Otherwise, you may abuse the privilege and devalue it.

Self-Reflection

I challenge you to surrender to God. Then as you pray, you will be transformed through prayer.

Adult Journal (Share your thoughts)

_____

_____

_____

_____

_____

_____

_____

_____

_____

<u>*A Prophetic Point*</u>

Pray as though He can only hear when it's coming from your heart!

<u>*Prayer*</u>

Lord, help us to develop our own private, intimate and personal relationship with you. Build it on our trust in you. We know that you know everything about us and that only you can help us. Lord, help our family depend on you.

Lesson #25 - "Praise & Worship"

The Bible (Scripture)

Come, let us sing for joy to the LORD; let us shout aloud to the Rock of our salvation. Let us come before him with thanksgiving and extol him with music and song. For the LORD is the great God, the great King above all gods. In his hand are the depths of the earth, and the mountain peaks belong to him. The sea is his, for he made it, and his hands formed the dry land. Come, let us bow down in worship, let us kneel before the LORD our Maker; for he is our God and we are the people of his pasture, the flock under his care. (Psalm 95:1-7 NIV)

A Prophetic Word

We sing, and shout our praise to God. We kneel down and bow in worship to God. We approach God with thanksgiving, with music and songs. We acknowledge our King, His greatness, and His sovereignty over all creation. We depend on God. He takes good care of us and He deserves the acclaim of His people.

Self-Reflection

There are moments in time when you must forget your life and everything in it. Give those moments to God. Now praise God. For He deserves it!

Adult Journal (Share your thoughts)

_____

_____

_____

_____

_____

_____

_____

_____

_____

_____

_____

A Prophetic Point

God is great amazing powerful and wonderful. Everything God creates reveal this too. You are a part of his creation. Created thing that is great, yield to the creator who is greater!

Poem

We come singing, shouting

We start kneeling and bowing

Our hearts move into worship of the Lord our God

When we focus on you

We praise you for all you've done

And we hope in the things you will do

We live to serve the King of Kings -

Who reigns with dominion and power

In our hearts, sweet melodies ring

Until your glory showers

Amen

Lesson #26 - "Service & Fellowship"

They preached the gospel in that city and won a large number of disciples. Then they returned to Lystra, Iconium and Antioch, strengthening the disciples and encouraging them to remain true to the faith. "We must go through many hardships to enter the kingdom of God," they said. Paul and Barnabas appointed elders for them in each church and, with prayer and fasting, committed them to the Lord, in whom they had put their trust. After going through Pisidia, they came into Pamphylia, and when they had preached the word in Perga, they went down to Attalia. From Attalia they sailed back to Antioch, where they had been committed to the grace of God for the work they had now completed. On arriving there, they gathered the church together and reported all that God had done through them and how he had opened a door of faith to the Gentiles. And they stayed there a long time with the disciples. (Acts 14:21-28 NIV)

A Prophetic Word

Paul and Barnabas preached the gospel to people believed and were converted. They strengthened believers in other churches. They appointed elders to serve. Then they returned to Antioch to tell all that God had done and they spent time with the other disciples. There was a time for service and a time for fellowship. There is a time for everything, and a season for every activity under the heavens. Be sure you are anchored in service and equally in fellowship. For it is in service that you develop relationship with other believers. It is through fellowship that you strengthen the bonds with others and become family.

Self-Reflection

Evaluate your service vs. fellowship relationship. Is it balanced? Fix it!

Adult Journal (Share your thoughts)

_____

_____

_____

_____

_____

_____

_____

A Prophetic Point

If you want to see God, share the gospel, strengthen other Christians and grow together in faith.

Poem

Our leaders walk with the Lord
They study, pray, and proclaim the truth
Then extend invitations to discipleship
And to join the kingdom with you

They encourage us all to stay committed
And endure the hard times we hate
This is how God builds the ministry
To assist our journey of faith

God calls men and women
And reveals whose been called
They are disciplined, and prepared in advance,
Strengthened to overcome a fall

Strengthened to fight the enemy
Strengthened not to quit
Strengthened infinitely
To be spiritually fit

With prayer and fasting, they are later chosen
And appointed somewhere to serve
We all share the gospel outside
And to support other Christians in the church
This is the service in the ministry Amen!

Stage 9 - Loving obedience

<u>Lesson #27 - Love I</u>

The Bible (Scripture)

Hearing that Jesus had silenced the Sadducees, the Pharisees got together. One of them, an expert in the law, tested him with this question: "Teacher, which is the greatest commandment in the Law?" Jesus replied: "'Love the Lord your God with all your heart and with all your soul and with all your mind. This is the first and greatest commandment. And the second is like it: 'Love your neighbor as yourself.' All the Law and the Prophets hang on these two commandments." (Matthew 22:34-39 NIV)

A Prophetic Word

Chief priests, elders, Pharisees and Sadducees have repeatedly questioned the Lord. He told many parables and answered their questions, scolding them for their unbelief, and evil hearts. When they asked Jesus which is the greatest commandment in the Law, He once again called out their place of err, telling them to love the Lord their God.

Of course they did not love the Lord their God. They didn't know the Lord, couldn't love Him, and wouldn't exhaust their heart, soul or mind loving him. Nevertheless, it is the beginning of all commandments and the most important. The other commandments in the law were supposed to reveal that man needed God's help to fulfill them. The law fulfilled would reveal a love for God and each other. The greater revelation is that God loved us enough to help us, sending his son in live and His spirit of love to help us love. For that, we should respond to God with love. That is good enough reason to love others.

Self-Reflection

I challenge you to think on the how God's love is changing your life. Now think on how you can change someone else's life if they receive love from you.

Adult Journal (Share your thoughts)

_____

_____

_____

_____

_____

_____

_____

A Prophetic Point

Your love displayed will help others look for the greater source. Start the search now!

Prayer

Heavenly Father, teach us to love you, your people. You have a way of creating people the way they are, accepting them where they are, and developing them into who they are supposed to become. Help us to see others through your eyes and love them as much as possible. Amen!

Lesson #28 - Love II

The Bible (Scripture)

And now these three remain: faith, hope and love. But the greatest of these is love. (1 Corinthians 13:13)

A Prophetic Word

When we were created, we were created to love. It was an act of love. We were created by love, for love. Anything done with a different motive is fruitless.

Self-Reflection

Focus on the depth of God's loving sacrifice for you and on your loving devotion to God. Then live out that loving devotion in all you do.

Adult Journal (Share your thoughts)

_____

_____

_____

_____

_____

_____

_____

A Prophetic Point

Love saved you. Now let God's love do the living in your life.

Poem

Faith unlocks the door

Hope sees what's on the other side

Love holds my agenda, my relationships, my destiny, and the will of God for my

life

Lesson #29 - Obedience

Scripture

"Before long, the world will not see me anymore, but you will see me. Because I live, you also will live. On that day you will realize that I am in my Father, and you are in me, and I am in you. 21 Whoever has my commands and keeps them is the one who loves me. The one who loves me will be loved by my Father, and I too will love them and show myself to them." John 14:19-21

A Prophetic Word

Jesus was explaining to his disciples that God is with them now (in Jesus), in the future coming of the Holy Spirit. The good news is that if you love and receive Jesus as Lord and Savior then you will have access to the Father who will send you the Holy Spirit as your comforter. Through the Holy Spirit, God will live with you and continue to be with you. Jesus insisted that the people of the world would no longer see him anymore but the disciples would spiritually recognize Jesus and be connected to Him. Jesus encourages us that if we love Him, we will obey His commands. Though today, we cannot see Him, we are inspired by His story, convicted by His word and willing to obey His commands.

Self-Reflection

When there is a fire, we are instructed to stop, drop and roll. The need for obedience is an emergency. Stop drop and seek God. Then obey God!

A Prophetic Point

I challenge you to obey His every prompting. God will respond to obedient love with more love.

Poem

Who can see me?

Others cannot see me

But you can

Who is in me?

Others are not in me

But you are

Who is in Christ?

I live in Christ

Since you are in me, you will live in Christ

Who is in the Father?

Since I am in the father and you are in me, then you are in the father

Who is in you?

Since the Holy Spirit is in you, then I am inside of you, and the father too

Who loves me?

Whoever is in me, loves me

You must obey me to be in me

If you obey me, then you love me

Who loves you?

I love you.

Love me and I will love you more

Our father will love you

We will live in you and love you even more

Stage 10 - Suffering Affliction

Lesson #30 - Suffering

The Bible (Scripture)

For those who are led by the Spirit of God are the children of God. The Spirit you received does not make you slaves, so that you live in fear again; rather, the Spirit you received brought about your adoption to sonship. And by him we cry, *"Abba,* Father." The Spirit himself testifies with our spirit that we are God's children. Now if we are children, then we are heirs—heirs of God and co-heirs with Christ, if indeed we share in his sufferings in order that we may also share in his glory. (Romans 8:14-17 NIV)

A Prophetic Word

The writer of Romans wants us to understand that the leading of the spirit is the key. That very act of obediently surrendering and following solidifies us as children of God, adopted sons, co-heirs with Christ. We will be rewarded with both suffering and glory. Trouble will visit you in many forms. It may frustrate you and cause emotional pain. Accidents and erosion will cause you financial trouble. Temporary darkness will cause you spiritual complacency. Unawareness of new challenges may tempt you to wallow in fear or worry. You however, have the opportunity to grow to new heights in faith.

Self-Reflection

Do you fear the thought of suffering? Praise God now for both suffering and glory.

Adult Journal (Share your thoughts)

_____

_____

_____

_____

_____

_____

_____

_____

_____

A Prophetic Point

In Christ, you are a prisoner of war, promoted to General! You will suffer but you will never lose the battle!

Prayer

Father, send your spirit to fill us again

Remind us that Jesus is a friend.

Let us follow the way

Obey and do what the spirit say

Children of the King,

Accept our prayer

Teach us to walk and live as heirs

<u>Lesson #31 - Maturity & Resilience</u>

The Bible (Scripture)

You, however, know all about my teaching, my way of life, my purpose, faith, patience, love, endurance, persecutions, sufferings—what kinds of things happened to me in Antioch, Iconium and Lystra, the persecutions I endured. Yet the Lord rescued me from all of them. In fact, everyone who wants to live a godly life in Christ Jesus will be persecuted, while evildoers and impostors will go from bad to worse, deceiving and being deceived. But as for you, continue in what you have learned and have become convinced of, because you know those from whom you learned it, and how from infancy you have known the Holy Scriptures, which are able to make you wise for salvation through faith in Christ Jesus. All Scripture is God-breathed and is useful for teaching, rebuking, correcting and training in righteousness, so that the servant of God may be thoroughly equipped for every good work. (2 timothy 3:10-17)

A Prophetic Word

The apostle Paul suffered for living and preaching the gospel. He has lived long enough to know that the Lord will rescue you. Yet the Lord rescued me from all of them. The word of the Lord proclaimed through Paul is to stay committed to the Lord, be resilient and keep progressing on your track to maturity. There are more ways for you to serve the Lord and more ways for you to grow as you learn and use God's word.

Self-Reflection

As for you, I challenge you to stand strong against everything that hinders you from walking in faith in Christ Jesus. Proclaim prophetically in advance how you will stand!

Adult Journal (Share your thoughts)

_____

_____

_____

_____

_____

_____

_____

A Prophetic Point

Stand against it or be enslaved to it. You choose!

Poem

You know my way
What God requires

The truth I teach
How I aspire

The way I live
And handle stress

The faith in me
That keeps me blessed

The way I wait,
How I go through

These things
I expect of you

In life you'll often see the mark
Then you'll seem so far apart

If you should fall and start to thirst
Go back to what you've learned at first

A holy God saved sinful you
When you had no chance, had no clue

He called your name, reached out His hand
And saved you from the sinking sand

Just call His name again my friend
He will return, remove your sin

Heal your soul, restore your life
He'll do it once, do it twice

Just recall the sacrifice -
It's of the Lord who is the Christ

The cross, the blood
The will of God, eternal love

All worked for you
Now you should know

You can bounce back
You will grow

Seek the Lord in love, in Haste
Salvation comes to those with faith!

Stage 11 – Glory

Lesson #32 - The Glory of God

The Bible (Scripture)

Praise be to the God and Father of our Lord Jesus Christ, who has blessed us in the heavenly realms with every spiritual blessing in Christ. For he chose us in him before the creation of the world to be holy and blameless in his sight. In love he predestined us for adoption to sonship through Jesus Christ, in accordance with his pleasure and will— to the praise of his glorious grace, which he has freely given us in the one he loves. In him we have redemption through his blood, the forgiveness of sins, in accordance with the riches of God's grace that he lavished on us. With all wisdom and understanding, he made known to us the mystery of his will according to his good pleasure, which he purposed in Christ, to be put into effect when the times reach their fulfillment—to bring unity to all things in heaven and on earth under Christ. In him we were also chosen, having been predestined according to the plan of him who works out everything in conformity with the purpose of his will, in order that we, who were the first to put our hope in Christ, might be for the praise of his glory. And you also were included in Christ when you heard the message of truth, the gospel of your salvation. When you believed, you were marked in him with a seal, the promised Holy Spirit, who is a deposit guaranteeing our inheritance until the redemption of those who are God's possession—to the praise of his glory. (Ephesians 1:3-14 NIV)

A Prophetic Word

We are blessed, chosen, predestined, granted redemption, forgiven, included in Christ, marked with a seal, guaranteeing our inheritance. This is all for the praise of his glory. To God be the glory.

God established a spiritual blessing in Christ for us that we don't understand. As we grapple with spiritual truths, and walk by faith, we grow in grace and become holy just like Him. This is His will in Christ Jesus.

Self-Reflection

Whatever you are going through, I remind you to remember the message of truth, the gospel of your salvation.

Then think on the Lord who made available to you all that you have in Christ, all that the spirit brings to you.

Adult Journal (Share your thoughts)

_____

_____

_____

_____

_____

_____

_____

_____

_____

_____

_____

A Prophetic Point

Know that your circumstances are small compared to the glory of God. God will sustain you in your circumstance and despite your circumstance. Your faith and your persistence contributes to His glory. Stay in the faith and stay encouraged. It will all come to pass.

Poem

The God of heaven has a blessing to share
It is a spiritual gift, it is truly rare

It is for those who have faith,
Who'll become holy?

Children, adopted by grace

It's time to get it, just hope for it, you'll feel it
If you're sealed with the Spirit, then God will reveal it.

We have a trust fund worth of gifts of God
He will let us redeem them in time.

Lesson #33 - Christ formed in you

The Bible (Scripture)

Now I rejoice in what I am suffering for you, and I fill up in my flesh what is still lacking in regard to Christ's afflictions, for the sake of his body, which is the church. I have become its servant by the commission God gave me to present to you the word of God in its fullness— the mystery that has been kept hidden for ages and generations, but is now disclosed to the Lord's people. To them God has chosen to make known among the Gentiles the glorious riches of this mystery, which is Christ in you, the hope of glory. He is the one we proclaim, admonishing and teaching everyone with all wisdom, so that we may present everyone fully mature in Christ. To this end I strenuously contend with all the energy Christ so powerfully works in me. (Colossians 1:24-29 NIV)

A Prophetic Word

The apostle Paul is writing about suffering for the sake of the church. Paul said this is his duty or service. He was completely devoted to serve and to not be self-centered, or egocentric. As we mature in the church, our responsibility should be to serve, to be an example of Christ.

Self-Reflection

I challenge you to share the story and the love of Jesus Christ. He lives in us. He is our everything!

Adult Journal (Share your thoughts)

_____

_____

_____

_____

_____

_____

_____

_____

_____

_____

_____

_____

_____

_____

A Prophetic Point

You cannot fathom or imagine what you will become. God will see it and say well done!

Poem

The Lord prepares preachers to proclaim the word of God

The word is rich and full to mature the church at large

The truth of God proclaimed, the mystery, Christ in you

To build us up, to encourage and to mature us too

The servants suffer, agonize, but rejoice along the way

Working diligently to serve the church and see the mighty day

To see the goal, you made whole

That's what ends the story

Christ in you, will unfold

That's the hope of glory

Journey of Faith Ministries

ABOUT THE AUTHOR

Dr. Derrick L Randolph, Sr. is from Baltimore, Maryland.

www.ingramcontent.com/pod-product-compliance
Lightning Source LLC
Chambersburg PA
CBHW021208020426
42331CB00003B/258